Sharon Turner thank you
for your support.

Jat Bleak

LIVING A HOLY SINGLE LIFE

JUANITA M. BULLOCK

authorHOUSE®

AuthorHouse™
1663 Liberty Drive
Bloomington, IN 47403
www.authorhouse.com
Phone: 1-800-839-8640

First published by AuthorHouse 12/9/2011

ISBN: 978-1-4520-7137-4 (sc)
ISBN: 978-1-4567-5505-8 (e)

Library of Congress Control Number: 2010912302

Printed in the United States of America

Any people depicted in stock imagery provided by Thinkstock are models,
and such images are being used for illustrative purposes only.
Certain stock imagery © Thinkstock.

All Bible references are from the KJV Bible. Holman Bible
Publishers. Nashville TN 37234. Copyright 1979.

This book is printed on acid-free paper.

DEDICATION

First and foremost I give honor to God for everything He has done and is doing in my life. I dedicate this book to all single brothers and sisters who are striving to live a holy life. I thank God for spiritual guidance from my Pastor, Bishop Curtis E. Edmonds Sr. of St. Mark Missionary Baptist Church in Portsmouth, VA and former Pastor, Bishop James T. Farrow Sr. of Philadelphia Church of Christ's Disciples #2 in Chesapeake, VA. I sincerely dedicate a large portion of my work and journey to my God fearing mother, Pearl Gloria Lee Jones, and father, James Henry Jones Sr., whom are deceased but not forgotten. Thank you Lord for my brothers and sisters and their spouses: Rita Wilson (George), James Henry Jones Jr., Duanita Jones, Ivan Jones (Nicole), Rodney Jones (Kiki), Devonna Jones and Brian Jones. I truly thank God for my supportive in-laws, Larry Thomas Bullock Sr. (deceased) and Elizabeth Bullock, Gary and Dakita Bullock, Eric and Ebony Hudson. I thank God for the following contributors: Dellino Wilson, Cynthia Marshall, Zenora Spellman, Regina Kee, Thomasena Robinson, Jarvis and Felecia Thomas. I thank the following people for your ongoing support: Inez and Nathaniel Ruffin, Ernestia Williams, Latisha Wilson, Sharon Smith Barnes, Sonya Sparrow, Robert and Natalie Mayo, Yvette Johnson, Chris and Tonya Griffin, Charmaine Smith, Ebony Wilson and to all my nieces and nephews. Last but not least I dedicate this book to my husband and best friend Larry T. Bullock Jr. Thank you for your never-ending support.

ABOUT THE AUTHOR

Juanita M. Bullock, author, writer, speaker and missionary has been prepared by God to carry out all of her God given assignments. Juanita M. Bullock is the daughter of the late James Henry Sr. and Pearl Gloria Lee Jones. She is married to Larry T. Bullock Jr. of Portsmouth, Virginia. Mrs. Bullock is the proud parent of Jordan Larissa Bullock (deceased), Larry Thomas Bullock III and step parent of two beautiful daughters, Jazmyn Parker and Jayla Bullock. Mrs. Bullock is currently under the leadership of Bishop Curtis E. Edmonds Sr. at St. Mark Missionary Baptist Church in Portsmouth, VA. On February 1, 2002 she was ordained as a missionary under the leadership of Bishop James T. Farrow Sr. of Philadelphia Church of Christ's Disciples #2 in Chesapeake, VA. God has blessed her to receive two degrees from Norfolk State University. She obtained a Bachelor of Science Degree in Social Work May 1997 and a Master's Degree in Urban Education December 2001. She has been a guest speaker at church and civic functions, women's conferences, single's forums and youth programs.

MESSAGE FROM THE AUTHOR

I greet you in the name of Jesus. It is my honor to share with you my thoughts on paper while living holy and single. This book was written during the last six years of my single and holy walk with the Lord. All of the chapters were written during the midst of what I was experiencing at that time of my life. In the beginning of singleness I felt like the single journey I was traveling had no end. Lo and behold, I made it through a season of singleness and you will be able to do the same. God has blessed me to know Him intimately in singleness. I am praying that after reading this book you will run the race of singleness with much zeal. I encourage you to read and share this book with a friend. I am certain you will be blessed. J.B.

TABLE OF CONTENTS

CHAPTER 1

HOLINESS

Holy – consecrated or devoted to the service of God.

For I am the Lord your God: ye shall therefore sanctify yourselves, and ye shall be holy; for I am holy: neither shall ye defile yourselves with any manner of creeping thing that creepeth upon the earth. For I am the Lord that bringeth you up out of the land of Egypt, to be your God: ye shall therefore be holy, for I am holy. **Leviticus 11: 44-45**

God is Holy. The creatures in heaven never stop saying holy. The Bible says, "And the four beasts had each of them six wings about him; and they were full of eyes within: and they rest not day and night, saying, holy, holy, holy. Lord God Almighty, which was, and is, and is to come" Revelation 4:8. Holiness is the standard of living for God. In order to be successful at being holy you must devote your life and daily living to pleasing God. God is our model of holiness. As holy men and women you have to desire to please God wholeheartedly. Jesus was completely holy; therefore during each season of singleness we can identify with God's word and how it aides us into having a victorious life: "Having therefore these promises, dearly beloved, let us cleanse ourselves from all filthiness of the flesh and spirit, perfecting holiness in the fear of God" II Corinthians 7:1.

God does not force holiness upon us. Holiness is obtained through ongoing persistence to please God. Everyone will give an account of the life they live. As a single man or woman you have to make a choice.

Will you allow the enemy to dangle you around like a puppet; as if he had power over you or will you allow God to receive the glory out of your season of singleness? The pursuit of happiness lies in holiness. The Israelites were given a choice. The Bible says, "And if it seem evil unto you to serve the Lord, choose you this day whom ye will serve; whether the gods which your fathers served that were on the other side of the flood, or the gods of the Amorites, in whose land ye dwell: but as for me and my house, we will serve the Lord. And the people answered and said, God forbid that we should forsake the Lord, to serve other gods: For the Lord our God, He it is that brought us up and our fathers out of the land of Egypt, from the house of bondage, and which did those great signs in our sight, and preserved us in all the way wherein we went, and among all the people through whom we passed. And the Lord drave out from before us all the people, even the Amorites which dwelt in the land: therefore will we also serve the Lord; for He is our God" Joshua 24:15-18.

The Lord says, "Behold, I set before you the way of life, and the way of death" Jeremiah 21:8. Holiness is about making a choice. When Elijah was on Mount Carmel, He called for the Israelites to make a decision: "And Elijah came unto all the people, and said, How long shalt ye be between two opinions? If the Lord be God, follow Him: but if Baal, then follow him. And the people answered him not a word" I King 18:21. Jesus comes with the truth about salvation and the eternal gains while in comparison, satan disguises the way to hell with bells and whistles. Isn't that typical of satan? Satan never comes boldly with the truth: "There is a way which seemeth right unto a man, but the end thereof are the ways of death" Proverbs 14:12. Holiness is required. There is a difference between holy standards and ungodly standards. Sin separates us from God. A little sin can be seen by God. In the sight of God a little sin is too much sin.

The Bible says, "Know ye not that a little leaven leaveneth the whole lump? Purge out therefore the old leaven, that ye may be a new lump, as ye are unleavened. For even Christ our passover is sacrificed for us: Therefore let us keep the feast, not with old leaven, neither with the leaven of malice and wickedness; but with the unleavened bread of sincerity and truth" I Corinthians 5: 6-8. Leaven is defined as an agent such as yeast that causes batter or dough to rise.

I recall a minister giving a sermon regarding a little leaven. The minister spoke about a woman who made a batch of cookies. Within the ingredients she places a teaspoon of cow dung in the mixture. The minister stated, "no matter how little cow dung she places in the mixture it destroyed the entire batch." Just like sin, too little sin is too much in the sight of God. God cannot tolerate sin. Whether it is one sin or multiple sins, transgressing against God's law displeases Him. When the lights are out or when we are behind closed doors do we display holiness?

The Bible says, "Let your light so shine before men, that they may see your good works, and glorify your Father which is in heaven" Matthew 5:16. We will either abide by God's law or disobey it. There is no such thing as fulfilling parts of God's law. God's law must be abided by in totality. God's law is His ruling. God says, "If ye love me, keep my commandments" John 14:15. Jesus says, "He that hath my commandments, and keepeth them, he it is that loveth me: and he that loveth me shall be loved of my Father, and I will love him, and will manifest myself to him" John 14:21. The choice is ours. We have to position ourselves to be in agreement with God regarding all things, not some things. While serving God we must have a yes disposition. Yes to your will. Yes to your way. Yes I will go. Yes I will obey. We will never be in a position to blame God for the choices we make. God established in the beginning freedom to obey His word. He has never forced anyone to serve Him.

The Bible says, "Enter ye in at the strait gate: for wide is the gate and broad is the way, that leadeth to destruction, and many there be which go in thereat: Because strait is the gate, and narrow is the way, which leadeth unto life, and few there be that find it" Matthew 7:13-14. Jesus declares the way. Jesus says, "I am the way, the truth, and the life: no man cometh unto the Father, but by me" John 14:6. Holiness sets us apart from satan. God is holy and everything connected to Him is holy. We can't begin to please the Lord until holiness is obtained and embedded in our heart. There is no such thing as partial holiness. God is looking for devoted men and women who will deny themselves to please Him. Even though we are very special to God, He will not tamper with our judgment to serve Him. Living holy on purpose will develop purification of the mind and spirit. Man must be a willing participant in his own holiness.

Our purpose must be straightforward. We must take up our cross and follow Christ. Jesus said, "If any man will come after me, let him deny himself, and take up his cross daily, and follow me. For whosoever will save his life shall lose it: but whosoever will lose his life for my sake, the same shall save it. For what is a man advantaged, if he gain the whole world, and lose himself, or be cast away?" Matthew 16:24. The kingdom of God is inside of us, so we can be holy. The Bible says, "Now when He was asked by the Pharisees when the kingdom of God would come, He answered them and said, "The kingdom of God does not come with observation; nor will they say, 'See here!' or 'See there!' For indeed, the kingdom of God is within you" Luke 17:20-21. One must work diligently to be holy. We must work harder on this job than any job we've ever had.

God told Israel to be distinct from the other nations by giving them specific governing rules. Israel will always be known for being God's chosen people. God commanded the Israelites to live by His holy standard which clearly identified them as the chosen generations.

The Bible says, "But ye are a chosen generation, a royal priesthood, an holy nation, a peculiar people: that ye should shew forth the praises of Him who hath called you out of darkness into His marvelous light: Which in time past were not a people, but are now the people of God: which had not obtained mercy, but now have obtained mercy" I Peter 2:9-10. Holiness is a choice that we must accept or deny. It is required by God. Holiness should be characteristic of her every child of God. The church will be presented to God as pure. The Bible says, "That he might present it to himself a glorious church, not having a spot, or wrinkle, or any such thing; but that it should be holy and without blemish" Ephesians 5:27. A spot is representative of sin. The sinful nature of man is not pure. We can't claim that God is leading our life without surrendering our heart to holiness. God must lead us entirely. Being disobedient will separate us from God.

There are dangers acquainted with being separated by God. Satan was disobedient leading him to not only being demoted but also kicked out of heaven. We must make up our mind to live holy whether others are living holy or not. Holiness is required and is an important aspect of daily living for God. A person who exercises holiness is considered peculiar by the world's viewpoint. If we are considered peculiar to the world then of course we are familiar to Christ. Can you fathom God watching us from the throne as we partake in acts that are not holy? Even when you think no one is watching God sees it all. God is our model of holiness. Living holy requires effort. Don't just put forth an attempt to do right, do it. We are not going to by chance slip into heaven. I know we live in a world that is motivated by schemes, short cuts and just plain old getting over, but that does not settle well with God.

I can remember sneaking into older age clubs with a fake I.D. and fooling the doormen for access to enter. I can recall cheating on class assignments and receiving good grades. There has been an increase in fraud on all levels and people getting away with the swindle. Even some of the most intriguing and well thought out ways of worldly deceit fool men. The entry way to heaven will amazingly shock the rich man, the generous giver, the nice lady and many more. No one will be able to outwit or deceive the all knowing God. Failing to commit to serving the Lord will bring forth horrendous consequences. God loves mankind. He hates the sinful nature of man. The Bible says, "Herein is love, not that we loved God, but that he loved us, and sent his Son to be the propitiation for our sins" I John 4:10. Holiness is required for triumphant living for God. God wants to save the unrighteous.

The Bible says, "Behold, the Lord's hand is not shortened, That it cannot save: Nor His ear heavy, That it cannot hear. But your iniquities have separated you from God; And your sins have hidden His face from you, so that He will not hear" Isaiah 59:1-2. A child of God must experience their mind being transformed to His way: "And be not conformed to this world: but be ye transformed by the renewing of your mind, that ye may prove what is good, and acceptable, and perfect, will of God" Romans 12:2. Always remember God and satan cannot co-exist with one another to do great things. The two have been separated since satan's fall. The list below demonstrates some of the differences between living holy and unrighteous:

Holiness /The Narrow Gate

Least road traveled
Not popular
Holds accountability
Requires self-control
Clings to every word of the Lord
Considered lonely by the world's standard
God almighty is worshipped
The only way to God
Rewards a crown
Governed by rules
Believes every word of God
Disciplined lifestyle

Unrighteous/ The Broad Gate
Many travel
Is very popular
Utilized by many
Is the easy way out
Is highly acceptable by the world
Holds no accountability

Does not require a disciplined lifestyle
Aborts any part of God's word that does not mesh well with
the individual's lifestyle
Many gods are worshipped
Out of control

CHAPTER 2

IT'S ONLY A SEASON

Season – A period characterized by particular conditions of weather, temperature, any period of time.

To every thing there is a season, and a time to every purpose under the heaven: A time to be born, and a time to die; a time to plant, and a time to pluck up that which is planted; A time to kill, and a time to heal; a time to break down and a time to build up; A time to weep, and a time to laugh; a time to mourn, and a time to dance; A time to cast away stones, and a time to gather stones together; a time to embrace, and a time to refrain from embracing; A time to get, and a time to lose; a time to keep, and a time to cast away; A time to rend, and a time to sew; a time to keep silence, and a time to speak; A time to love, and a time to hate; a time of war, and a time of peace. Ecclesiastes 3: 1-8

Seasons reflect a beginning and a end. Seasons gracefully welcome one another. God is an on time God who works wonders in every season. There has never been a time in history that winter, spring, summer or fall failed to show up before any calendar year was out. I know you have experienced seasonal changes whereby the summer felt like the spring and the spring felt like the fall. For years meteorologists have been thrown off from reasonable predictions as it pertain to the credibility of their weather reports. Often weather reports indicate rain but God allows sunshine. No one, not even you can say when your season will begin or end. But do you know why we change seasons? It's all in the tilt! While it may seem that the seasons are caused by the earth's changing distance from the sun, it's really due to the tilt of the earth's axis. This tilt–a 23-degree slant-enables the sun to appear above the horizon for different lengths of time at different seasons.

Seasons changing indicate that there may be a tilt of the earth's axis but the sun is always present. The tilt determines whether the sun's rays strike at a low angle or more directly. In all seasons the sun is apparent. Just like our heavenly Father. God is present during every season of our lives. Change is inevitable. God wants you to be hopeful. God determines your change. Always keep in mind that if you try to shorten your season with your so called bright plan the results for doing so could be very damaging. During any season we must let patience grow in our life. We can't calculate how long this season will last so work hard for the Lord and be patient until a change comes. Satan couldn't stop us from entering into a new season that is directed by God.

Whether we believe seasons last or not a change is coming. As a child of God we must anticipate change. We may feel like we are an occupant in the winter but be assured of one thing, the summer is coming. God and the phrase out of season never align itself with one another. In the meantime prepare for a change. Prepare means set up, get ready, put in order and make ready. If Jesus says that He has to go away to prepare a place for you, then you must recognize the preparation time is often a good sign: "And if I go and prepare a place for you, I will come again, and receive you to myself; that where I am, there you may be also" John 14:3. With that in mind, do not trouble yourself with the cares of this world.

The parable of the ten virgins is a great example of preparing for the greatest day of your life. The Bible says, "Then shall the kingdom of heaven be likened unto ten virgins, which took their lamps, and went forth to meet the bridegroom. And five of them were wise, and five were foolish. They that were foolish took their lamps, and took no oil with them: But the wise took oil in their lamps. While the bridegroom tarried they all slumbered and slept. And at midnight there was a cry made, Behold, the bridegroom cometh; go out to meet Him. Then all those virgins arose, and trimmed their lamps. And the foolish said unto the wise, Give us of your oil; for our lamps are gone out. But the wise answered, saying, Not so; lest there be not enough for us and you; but go ye rather to them that sell, and buy for yourselves. And while they went to buy, the bridegroom came; and they that were ready went in with him to the marriage: and the door shut. Afterward came also the other virgins, saying, Lord, Lord, open to us.

But he answered and said, Verily I say unto you, I know you not. Watch therefore, for ye know neither the day nor the hour wherein the Son of man cometh" Matthew 25: 1-13.

This parable teaches everyone to be ready at all times. Throughout the Bible it is clear that all the maidens appeared to be alike: they all took their lamps, they were all virgins, and they were all prepared to meet the bridegroom. What distinguishes the wise from the foolish virgins was the preparation phase. The five wise virgins prepared themselves for an extended wait on the Lord, while the foolish virgins prepared for a shorter period. They failed to anticipate the duration of the delay. All the virgins knew He was coming, but only a few could undergo the task of waiting. Preparation for eternal glory and gain while on earth requires patience and long suffering. It is imperative that you learn to prepare for the finale.

Be like those readily waiting for the Lord when He returns from the wedding in the book of Luke. The Bible says, "And ye yourselves like unto men that wait for their Lord, when He will return from the wedding; that when He cometh and knocketh, they may open unto Him immediately. Blessed are those servants, whom the Lord when He cometh shall find watching: verily I say unto you, that he shall gird himself, and make them to sit down to meat, and will come forth and serve them. And if He shall come in the second watch, or come in the third watch and find so, blessed are those servants. And this know, that if the good man of the house had known what hour the thief would come, he would have watched, and not have suffered his house to be broken through. Be ye therefore ready also: for the Son of man cometh at an hour when ye think not. Then Peter said unto him Lord, speakest thou this parable unto us, or even to all? And the Lord said, Who then is that faithful and wise steward, whom his lord shall make ruler over his household, to give them their meat in due season?" Luke 12: 36-42.

I know during seasons there will be numerous moments of frustration devised by satan to throw you off course. This is just a grand trick devised by satan. This attack will focus on alleviating contentment in being single. Of course during the waiting period our mind will be challenged in remaining content or not. During this season you can experience God being with you to fill the void. Whether you feel God's presence or not, He is there in this season. This stage will warrant being in God's presence and in return being highly blessed. What you will experience in crucial moments to hear from God will be sounding and awe inspiring. <u>God is Omnipresent. He is everywhere at the same time</u>. The Bible says, "Whither shall I go from Thy spirit? or whither shall I flee from Thy presence? If I ascend up into heaven, thou art there: if I make my bed in hell, behold, thou art there. If I take the wings of the morning, and dwell in the uttermost parts of the sea; Even there shall Thy hand lead me, and Thy right hand shall hold me. If I say, surely the darkness shall cover me; even the night shall be light about me. Yea, the darkness hideth not from thee; but the night shineth as the day: the darkness and the light are both alike to thee" Psalm 139:7-12.

After a while, many single men and women begin to think God isn't hearing their prayers and cries. God does hear you. <u>God is Omniscient. He knows everything that you are experiencing in this season</u>. The Bible says, "O LORD, thou hast searched me, and known me. Thou knowest my downsitting and mine uprising, thou understandest my thought afar off. Thou compassest my path and my lying down, and art acquainted with all my ways. For there is not a word in my tongue, but, lo, O LORD, thou knowest it altogether. Thou hast beset me behind and before, and laid thine hand upon me. Such knowledge is too wonderful for me; it is high, I cannot attain unto it" Psalm 139:1-6. There is no record in scripture that says God is hard of hearing and does not fulfill His promises. He is always there to listen and comfort us. Whenever we call on God be assured He hears us and will respond. When doubt enters our mind about God not being there for us read His word. You can't hear from God if you do not engage Him: "So then faith comes by hearing, and hearing by the word of God" Romans 10: 17.

We can't give the enemy footage over our lives. Singleness can be difficult at times, but you are equipped to stay the course. "Weeping may endure for a night but joy cometh in the morning" Psalm 30:5. Think back on a season when you wanted God to move on your behalf. As you reflect, remember how it took some time before you saw the fruits of your request? God blesses us over and over again. How soon we forget about how He brought us out of a situation that appeared to be such a long time ago? God hasn't changed. He is still in the business of blessing His children. God blesses us because He loves us.

Seasons sometimes warrant concerns. God does not want His children to be concerned about any situation. The Bible says, "Let not your heart be troubled: ye believe in God, believe also in me" John 14:1. God wants us to rest assure on His promises. We can't allow ourselves to be bothered about a situation that is out of our control.

You must channel our frustration into serving during this opportunist stage of spiritual development. During this season become great by taking on a disposition as a servant. God takes great delight in our efforts to become a good steward. Strive to be a patient steward. Patience is a virtue worth obtaining and retaining. The Bible says, "Knowing this, that the trying of your faith worketh patience. But let patience have her perfect work, that ye may be perfect and entire and wanting nothing" James 1:3-4. Faith and patience go hand and hand. We cannot serve God in fullness if we lack the ability to be patient. If you are anything like me, you may think about timing every so often during singleness. I did ask the Lord about experiencing companionship. I would make comments like: Lord what about me? Lord how long will you make me wait? Lord did you forget about me? At some point in my walk I realized that this walk was not tailored for self-fulfillment. God does not want us walking single and self centered. God wants to be the center of our life. God knows everything. He knows when your season of singleness is over. You just have to hold on and hang in there.

During this singleness season you will have challenges. These challenges can be called roller coaster rides. These roller coaster rides that you may experience could be brought on by satan or even yourself. I promise you there will be bumps in the road along the way so buckle your holy belt and enjoy the ride. You know satan is not stable in his own mind. Why shouldn't satan use roller coaster ride tactics as a weapon of attack if that ploy worked for him in the past? Why shouldn't satan revert back to a trick he used in the past when it proved to be successful for him. Satan can't think of new tricks during any season of your life. Satan uses old tricks because it works well for him. He skips around old tricks with new themes and fresh faces hoping to pull the wool over our eyes. Take an assessment of what the enemy has used in the past to tempt you. The enemy lurks in areas of our life where he thinks we are vulnerable. Then he attempts to test us in every area whereby we appear to be strong.

Nothing satisfies satan more than depleting strength from the strong at heart. Satan is characterized as being repetitious. Most often we discover that the same test has reoccurred in our life with a fresh face yet it has a similar theme. Some tests are given over to see if we've retained what we previously learned. A lot of times we need a refresher course to reiterate and reinforce what we already know. You are not forgotten during this season. Being single does not always feel good, but the time spent with God discussing the matter is precious. God is a jealous God; therefore during this season give Him your undivided attention. "Do not worship any other god, for the Lord, whose name is Jealous, is a jealous God" Exodus 34:14. God wants you to take pleasure in being single and spending time with Him. Enjoyable memories come from this stage of spiritual maturity. There is no one else to call on but God when trying to fix a matter of the heart.

God knows the importance of companionship if that is what you desire. He ordains lawful relations between a man and a woman. Rest on His promises and take delight in fellowship with God. The outcome for waiting on God to bring to a close your season of singleness will amaze you. A season of waiting on God requires relinquishing thoughts, plans and individual desires. As a servant of God we must learn to take a backseat and let God guide us. Waiting on God can be difficult, yet so rewarding. Following God can only bring about unheard of results, blessings and testimonies. Following God and always positions you for greatness. Waiting in most cases are comparable to valley experiences. Valleys are elongated depressions between the uplands of hills and mountains that are followed by the course of a stream. Elongated can be defined as being lengthy. Valleys can be lengthy, yet peace is attainable for the duration of the wait.

The Bible says, "Even though I walk through the valley of the shadow of death, I will fear no evil, for you are with me; your rod and your staff, they comfort me" Psalm 23:4. In essence this means be not fearful and allow God to guide you through singleness. You don't have to fear being alone. Or fear God is not working on your behalf. This season may feel overwhelming but be assured that you can walk it out victoriously. We will always prevail if we hold on to God. Waiting and valleys can also be noted as dark places or gloomy times. When we push through those rough times God will receive the glory for giving us the ability to endure. Even in the midst of stormy times God exhibits His glory. Have you ever heard about the lily in the valley? It can be representative of our illuminating Jesus flourishing in the midst of dark moments of our life. The wonders of God will never be explained. The reward that awaits you for enduring will be breathtaking. Jesus will always give us an array of hope in times and moments that are dim. While waiting during this single season learn to spend time with God.

Cherish the time in the morning, afternoon and evening that we can spend with Him. We should want to talk and hear from God continually. Intimacy with God will be heightened when quality time is spent in His presence. The fullness of God will be experienced when you completely surrender it all. When we have Christ within there is no greater love. Love begins from the inside. Beauty will shine on the outside once the inward man is made whole. Single men and women are precious to God. During this period God should become your first love. When you fall in love with God there is an attraction about your inward man that you can't explain. You wake up feeling beautiful. There is no falling in love encounter like that of our Lord and Savior. This love will make you love yourself. This love will make us love our enemies and everybody around us. This love will provide complete satisfaction. Fall in love under new management.

When we take the focus off of ourselves and crave to get closer to God it pleases Him. Don't think for a second that we are going to automatically fall deeply in love with God without spending any time with Him. Beginning a relationship with God requires constant conversing. Put forth every effort in becoming encircled by the Lord. When we fall in love with God we won't find it problematic to follow His lead. God is looking for someone who remains steadfast. Purposeful lives are spearheaded by the Lord. As a child of God your total man must develop an obedient position to every request that He commands. By following His precepts you will fall head over heels in love with Him over and over again. Have you ever heard married couples speaking about loving their spouse in a greater way today than yesterday? It's because of the investment and time put into the relationship.

God is always seeking someone that will take gratification in pleasing. How important is God in your life during this season? Is God more important than your boyfriend, girlfriend, children, job, church duties, recreational activities, school or what highly interest you? Focusing on what is important to God will please Him greatly and the manifested blessings of doing so will astound you. If God is considered to be your Lord then He must lead over your thoughts, emotions, time and body. God must govern every part of you. Walking outside of this teaching will cause us to be distracted and possibly deluded by the enemy. Satan can have us so wrapped up in our own affairs that we fail to recognize what is important to God. The devil enjoys watching us wasting time and energy in matters that don't involve God. As a believer you can't allow yourself to be sidetracked by the enemy. Involving ourselves with God will have our desires brought into fruition. God's business is our business. God does not respond well or listen to excuses about why we aren't able to make His business our business.

God is fully aware of our daily responsibilities. God is also aware of the orchestrated 24-hour clock that He perfectly designed to get all that is required of us done in a day. This design flawlessly distinguishes between day and night, given hours for work, rest and worship. Learn to stay the course. Staying the course during any season requires a deep level of commitment. It means eliminating our own itinerary in order to fulfill God's will. We are journeymen working for God. Once we grasp that we are journeying for a better life now and later we will stay the course. Staying on course is going to be a journey of faith, and much more. This season will not last forever. We will be tried, tested, and pursued intensely by satan. But it is okay. Moses wandered in the wilderness for 40 years. This journey would not have lasted as long if all of the people following him weren't complaining and murmuring. Never once during the journey did they lack. They were able to eat, drink and were clothed throughout the period of their travels. Yet the people continuously complained. All those older complainers who followed Moses did not make it to the promise land. God did say save Caleb the son of Jephunneh, and Joshua the son of Nun. Their descendants however did make it.

The LORD spoke to Moses and Aaron, saying, "How long shall I bear with this evil congregation, which murmur against me? I have heard the murmurings of the children of Israel, which they murmur against me. Say unto them, As truly as I live, saith the LORD, as ye have spoken in mine ears, so will I do to you: Your carcases shall fall in this wilderness; and all that were numbered of you, according to your whole number, from twenty years old and upward which have murmured gainst me. Doubtless ye shall not come into the land, concerning which I sware to make you dwell therein, save Caleb the son of Jephunneh, and Joshua the son of Nun. But your little ones, which ye said should be a prey, them will I bring in, and they shall know the land which ye have despised. But as for you, your carcases, they shall fall in this wilderness. And your children shall wander in the wilderness forty years, and bear your whoredoms, until your carcases be wasted in the wilderness. After the number of the days in which ye searched the land, even forty days, each day for a year, shall ye bear your iniquities, even forty years, and ye shall know my breach of promise. I the LORD have said, I will surely do it unto all this evil congregation, that are gathered together against me: in this wilderness they shall be consumed, and there they shall die" Numbers 14:26-35.

Are you equipped to endure a season that will change? Single men and women enjoy your travels. This excursion is set up to be pleasurable but yet so many single people are miserable. This journey should be completed with peace of mind. Make up your mind to be at peace. The Bible says, "Peace I leave with you, my peace I give unto you: not as the world giveth, give I unto you. Let not your heart be troubled, neither let it be afraid" John 14:27. When my mind was preoccupied about being single I would listen to worship music. I knew I needed something uplifting entering my mind at the same time satan was tugging at it. I was determined to walk out singleness with peace of mind. Just depend on Jesus every step of the way. In the meantime be fruitful during this season.

The Bible says, "A certain man had a fig tree planted in his vineyard; and he came and sought fruit thereon, and found none. Then said he unto the dresser of his vineyard, Behold, these three years I come seeking fruit on this fig tree and find none: cut it down; why cumbereth it the ground? And he answering said unto him, Lord, let it alone this year also, till I shall dig about it, and dung it: And if it bear fruit, well: and if not, then after that thou shalt cut it down" Luke 13:6-9. In this parable the master came looking for fruit and found none. The tree was designed to produce in season. God is expecting us to be fruitful in every season of life. Enjoy your season of singleness and produce fruits while experiencing peace at the same time. Once this stage of your life is gone, you will never get it back.

CHAPTER 3

A CALL FOR CHASTENING

Chastening –training to act in accordance to rules.

And ye have forgotten the exhortation which speaketh unto you as unto children, My son, despise not thou the chastening of the Lord, nor faint when thou art rebuked of him: For whom the Lord loveth he chasteneth, and scourgeth every son whom he receiveth. If we endure chastening, God dealeth with you as with sons: for what son is he whom the father chasteneth not? But if ye be without chastisement, whereof all are partakers, then are ye bastards, and not sons. Furthermore we have had fathers of our flesh which corrected us, and we gave them reverence: shall we not much rather be in subjection unto the Father of spirits, and live? For they verily for a few days chastened us after their own pleasure; but he for our profit, that we might be partakers of his holiness. Now no chastening for the present seemeth to be joyous, but grievous: nevertheless afterward it yielded to the peaceable fruit of righteousness unto them which are exercised thereby. Wherefore lift up the hands which hang down, and the feeble knees; And make; straight paths for your feet, lest that which is lame be turned out of the way; but let it rather be healed. **Hebrews 12:5-11**

Chastening and discipline are synonymous of one another. Discipline means holding your body in complete subjection of God's will. Discipline is not a topic up for discussion. Discipline is the discussion. Will you discuss or subject yourself to God's mandate on your life to be disciplined? Subjecting your body to God is a characteristic of holiness. In order to please God you must allow God to purge and train us in righteousness. There is something special to be said about a single man or woman who has restricted their body for the Lord. Discipline does not just occur one morning when you wake up. It is spearheaded by the Lord and requires effort on our part.

Do you know that we merit God's favor when we walk a disciplined lifestyle? God is calling for holiness, which is obtained by disciplining the whole man. Don't expect this to be an impossible task. Living holy is possible. If God has called us into holiness then it can be achieved. The Bible says, "I can do all things through Christ which strengtheneth me" Philippians 4:13. Many people don't understand why a child of God is expected to walk in a disciplined manner. God makes a clear distinction between Himself and satan. We are required to walk holy because it sets us apart from satan and his kingdom. Remember since the beginning satan has always worked hard at differing from God. Lucifer was set apart in heaven. He wanted to exalt himself above God.

The Bible speaks of satan's grand position in heaven and his great fall from heaven: "Son of man, take up a lamentation upon the king of Tyrus, and say unto him, Thus saith the Lord GOD; Thou sealest up the sum, full of wisdom, and perfect in beauty.Thou hast been in Eden the garden of God; every precious stone was thy covering, the sardius, topaz, and the diamond, the beryl, the onyx, and the jasper, the sapphire, the emerald, and the carbuncle, and gold: the workmanship of thy tabrets and of thy pipes was prepared in thee in the day that thou wast created. Thou art the anointed cherub that covereth; and I have set thee so: thou wast upon the holy mountain of God; thou hast walked up and down in the midst of the stones of fire. Thou wast perfect in thy ways from the day that thou wast created, till iniquity was found in thee. By the multitude of thy merchandise they have filled the midst of thee with violence, and thou hast sinned: therefore I will cast thee as profane out of the mountain of God: and I will destroy thee, O covering cherub, from the midst of the stones of fire. Thine heart was lifted up because of thy beauty, thou hast corrupted thy wisdom by reason of thy brightness: I will cast thee to the ground, I will lay thee before kings, that they may behold thee. Thou hast defiled thy sanctuaries by the multitude of thine iniquities, by the iniquity of thy traffick; therefore will I bring forth a fire from the midst of thee, it shall devour thee, and I will bring thee to ashes upon the earth in the sight of all them that behold thee" Ezekiel 28: 12-18.

Chastening requires disconnecting ourselves from the world. If we are not walking under the authority of God then we are on one accord with the world. If we've made a sound decision to live under the authority of God then we are no longer a comrade of the world. So subjecting oneself to God's rule and authority brings us into fellowship with Him. God takes great pleasure in identifying His own. The world and its' servants are not controllable. They blindly walk out of control and are managed by satan who has committed his life to a three-fold purpose: to kill, steal, and destroy. The Bible says, "The thief cometh not, but for to steal, and to kill, and to destroy: I am come that they might have life, and that they might have it more abundantly" John 10:10. Satan is motivated by the ability to deceive the world and to destroy the saints. Therefore, it is his duty to tempt us into going against being disciplined. Did you hear what I said? Satan has the ability to deceive us into walking according to our flesh if we allow him control over our mind.

We are the authoritarian over the life we decide to live. Don't allow satan to swindle us out of rewards for being obedient to God. Be always mindful that satan is the father of deceit. If we have decided to live under God's covering then we cannot govern ourselves with the world. The Bible says, "I beseech you therefore, brethren, by the mercies of God, that ye present your bodies a living sacrifice, holy, acceptable unto God, which is your reasonable service. And be not conformed to this world: but be ye transformed by the renewing of your mind, that ye may prove what is that good, and acceptable, and perfect, will of God" Romans 12:1-2. Whether disciplined by God or not, destiny awaits all of us. Every man will be compensated for the life they live. If we fail to discipline ourselves under God's mandates we will miss out on having an abundant life. I don't think we really want to miss out on anything that the Lord would love to give us.

We must always consider the total disciplined man. We don't want to find ourselves in a position where we acknowledge one portion of God's word and reject another. If we take on that philosophy then we could be considered a double minded individual. The Bible says, "A double minded man is unstable in all his ways" James 1:8. God calls for single minded persons. I can recall a minister saying anything with two minds is a freak. God is calling for disciplined followers. Pleasing the Lord requires a disciplined lifestyle. Our daily devotions, thoughts, environment, and entertainment must be geared towards disciplining the whole man. Take an assessment of the life you're living. Do you choose to discipline yourself under God's leadership or satans? God will not have children of His running around with an unhinged mind and soul. Discipline yourself now or receive the consequences from your actions.

There are consequences to pay for walking outside of a disciplined lifestyle. A disciplined lifestyle should be the core of your stewardship to God. Living discipline should be the forerunner of our living holy testimony. Make up your mind to be successful in this area. In order to live holy we must govern our life by and through Jesus. We must have a made up mind. Satan fears the word discipline with God leading the way. Discipline will fuel all disciples for any battle.

Discipline requires power, resilience, and faith in God. Satan has an extreme dislike for disciplined men and women of God. Knowledge about being disciplined must be learned and retained during this single and holy race. Satan is afraid of you gaining understanding about the disciplined man or woman of God. Satan does not want you knowledgeable on any level; especially as it pertain to your spiritual man. The Bible says, "My people are destroyed for lack of knowledge: because thou hast rejected knowledge, I will also reject thee, that thou shalt be no priest to me: seeing thou hast forgotten the law of thy God, I will also forget thy children" Hosea 4:6.

The enemy is attacking single men and women because he frets the devoted lifestyle they are able to have. Satan does not want anyone disciplined on any level serving God. The disciplined single man has more time to commit to building the kingdom than those who are married. In the Bible Job is portrayed as a man with great faith and discipline. He was disciplined in his faith walk with God. Job had a made up mind to serve God in spite of misfortunes. He wasn't going to let anyone persuade him out of trusting God. Job had a wife who told him to curse God and also he had friends who questioned all that he was experiencing. The Bible says, "Then said his wife unto him, Dost thou still retain thine integrity? Curse God, and die" Job 2:9.

The flesh can be disciplined if held under subjection to God. We can eliminate a lot of hardships by walking in a disciplined manner. I know all of us have experienced at some point in our life walking it out our way. It could have been in a personal relationship, on the job, in church or somewhere relevant in your life. By doing so, we reaped the consequences from it. I don't know about you, but I don't want unnecessary hardships. Exercise living by the word of God. I know we will always be tempted to go against the grain of the word of God but we must learn how to take authority over our bodies. We have great authority over our body.

CHAPTER 4

RESIST TEMPTATION

Temptation – the act of tempting; enticement or alluring.

There is no temptation taken you but such as is common to man: but God is faithful, who will not suffer you to be tempted above that ye are able; but will with the temptation also make a way to escape, that ye may be able to bear it. **I Corinthians 10:13**

The Bible says, "Now the serpent was more subtil than any beast of the field which the Lord God had made. And he said unto the woman, Yea, hath God said, Ye shall not eat of every tree of the garden? And the woman said unto the serpent, We may eat of the fruit of the trees of the garden: But of the fruit of the tree which is in the midst of the garden, God hath said, Ye shall not eat of it, neither shall ye touch it, lest ye die. And the serpent said unto the woman, Ye shall not surely die: For God doeth know that in the day ye eat thereof, then your eyes shall be opened, and ye shall be as gods, knowing good and evil. And when the woman saw that the tree was good for food, and that it was pleasant to the eyes, and a tree to be desired to make one wise, she took of the fruit thereof, and did eat, and gave also unto her husband with her: and he did eat" Genesis 3:1-6.

Temptation existed in the beginning of time. Temptation was introduced in the Garden of Eden. When all was wonderful in this land of great delight, satan surfaced in the form of a serpent stating words to make Eve question whether there was more to the forbidden tree than what God spoke of. Satan's deceitful trick to mislead Adam and Eve lead to the fall of mankind. The devil's craftiness and approach to deceiving Adam and Eve was subtle yet alluring. Adam and Eve yielded to satan's trickery, but Jesus withstood temptation and triumphed over him. Christ leads by example. Jesus faced opposition and won the battle. As a disciple of Christ you can resist temptation. The Bible says, "Temptation is first conceived in the mind. Then when lust hath conceived, it bringeth forth sin: and sin, when it is finished, bringeth forth death" James 1:15.

When we ponder on unholy thoughts that satan brings to our mind sin is birthed. Children of God will definitely be tried with this old dirty flesh. Flesh says I want instant gratification. God commands that you flee from worldly desires. When your flesh speaks, speak back to it immediately with scripture. We cannot attempt to satisfy our body and mind. The world attempts to thrill the flesh. As a believer we must exterminate ploys of satan by building up our spiritual man. Sometimes we may think we are able to resist the flesh, but that is a trick of satan. We must never lose focus.

In the beginning God gave Adam and Eve independence. They had the ability to choose to obey or disobey. The decision to do right or wrong will be determined by the individual. We have to be mindful that we are the temple of the living God. The only decision is the right decision. The choices we make in life will determine the reward we shall reap. If we sow into kingdom building then we will gain heavenly rewards. If we sow into building satan's kingdom then we will reap unfulfilling rewards which lead to eternal condemnation. God will never beg or tug on an individual to subject his or herself to His authority. We must make a decision. The Bible says, "Nothing good dwells in the flesh. For I know that in me (that is, in my flesh,) dwelleth no good thing: for to will is present with me; but how to perform that which is good I find not" Romans 7:18.

Jesus was tested during His wilderness experience. The Bible says, "And Jesus being full of the Holy Ghost returned from Jordan, and was led by the Spirit into the wilderness. Being forty days tempted of the devil. And in those days he did eat nothing: and when they were ended, He afterward hungered. And the devil said unto him, If thou be the Son of God, command this stone that it be made bread. And Jesus answered him, saying, It is written, That man shall not live by bread alone, but by every word of God. And the devil, taking him up into an high mountain, shewed unto him all the kingdoms of the world in a moment of time. And the devil said unto him, All this power will I give thee, and the glory of them: for that is delivered unto me; and to whomsoever I will I give it. If thou therefore wilt worship me, all shall be thine. And Jesus answered and said unto him, Get thee behind me, satan: for it is written, Thou shalt worship the Lord thy God, and Him only shalt thou serve. And he brought him to Jerusalem, and set him on a pinnacle of the temple, and said unto him, If thou be the Son of God, cast thyself down from hence: For it is written, He shall give His angels charge over thee, to keep thee: And in their hands they shall bear thee up, lest at any time thou dash thy foot against a stone. And Jesus answering said unto him, It is said, Thou shalt not tempt the Lord thy God. And when the devil had ended all the temptation, he departed from Him for a season" Luke 4:1-13.

The Bible states, satan departed from Jesus for a season. Temptations come and go; therefore satan will always return with luring tactics. Jesus was tempted in the wilderness. Satan has no respect of persons by whom he attacks. Jesus is the son of God, yet satan could not resist tempting Him. How foolish? Temptation is nothing new, nor is the way you defeat satan. There is no newly designed way of fighting satan than that of fellowship with God and His word. God has infinite power; therefore His children are well equipped to fight anything that may come to bring destruction. The Bible says, "For we have not a high priest which cannot be touched with the feeling of our infirmities; but was in all points tempted like as we are, yet without sin" Hebrews 4:15. The first and last

Adam was both tempted by appetite and position. The man perfectly created from the earth fell easily when tempted by appetite and position; such as all who are born in iniquity. The second Adam, perfectly made from heaven was tempted by appetite and position, but stood firm on faith and received the victory.

We can clearly see that satan tried on three occasions to tempt Jesus. We must make up our mind to repetitiously defeat the enemy. The enemy is always trying to thrive in the area of temptation since it was the first trick that worked for his betterment. Satan can only do what we allow him to do. Temptation belongs to the devil. Temptation must be defeated. If we don't conquer and crucify the flesh, it will triumph over us. Flesh refers to the sinful nature of man. Strongholds concerning the flesh are established when we lose sight of God. A stronghold is literally what it says. It is a spiritual force that will hold you strong. It is considered to be like a stranglehold. God is characterized as having all power and who is powerful. Strongholds carry no weight to God. A stronghold is nothing for God. Walk with Him and turn over the clutch that hinders your spiritual growth. Believers must depend solely on God for strength during such times.

The flesh yearning to be satisfied is a natural feeling. We can't respond to the flesh. Our flesh has a strong appetite. Often times by yielding to the flesh we settle for less than what God is trying to give us. Don't settle. Clearly know the flesh yearns to be pleased. We will fall into sin if we attempt to make our flesh blissful. We can't compromise pleasing our flesh even for a moment. I speak from experience. I fell into the enemy's trap several times. I, with my little thinking felt I could handle holding someone's hand. I thought I could handle a little physical affection. Then I thought I could handle kissing the individual. Boy, was I wrong! Those so call methods of pleasing my flesh woke it up. My sleeping flesh woke up and craved more. Has anybody ever informed you that you can never satisfy the flesh? The flesh will always want more than it previously had.

Why put ourselves through the trouble of awakening our flesh. Our flesh does not understand the phrase "for an appointed time". Our flesh says it wants instant satisfaction. Our flesh wants to constantly coddle in pleasure. We might think there is nothing wrong with awakening the flesh with a little touching and a few sensual kisses. We might even believe some physical contact is necessary. We might also be that individual who believes in subjecting oneself to a body tease. Keep in mind if you taunt the flesh, the outcome could pilot sin. Remember the goal is to please God in every facet of your life, which means on a date, in your home, in secret, wherever. Many people whom we come in contact with might be holy, but strongly believe some touching or a little intimacy is okay. We can't compromise our belief for the sake of another individual. We must make it our business to please God, not man. If the individual you're involved with is genuinely interested in you then he or she will respect your wishes.

If your desire is to limit sensual and sexual contact in your relationship then your partner should respect your request.

If you don't stand for sanctity in the beginning of your relationship then it will be a little difficult enforcing sensual limitations later. It won't be impossible to resist, but it will be a little harder. Be like Enoch. The Bible says, "Enoch walked to please God" Hebrews 11:5. When we focus on resisting temptation but persist on some physical involvement then we open ourselves up for greater challenges with our flesh. If we fail to reduce our efforts to tame the flesh we will open a window for the devil's entrance. If we are drawn in by the devil we will find ourselves in a situation that will warrant a desperate need for escape. God has empowered us to crucify the flesh. Once we invite intimacy in our life on any level our flesh will no longer lie dormant. We can't please God and our flesh at the same time. It is impossible. Temptations entice and drive the flesh.

If we dabble in sin it could lead to fornication. The flesh has a strong appetite and it will always war against your spirit. The more we feed our flesh, the more our flesh desires. We should not prance around the enemy like David? David was a man after God's own heart, yet he fell into temptation. David took his eyes off of God and fell prey to temptation. David observed Bathsheba bathing and inquired of her. Even though David knew she was married he dared not to think about morals. David's flesh desired her. There was nothing Godly about the decisions he made. David had allowed his mind to drift off in lust which resulted in sinning against his body. David committed a double sin. He committed adultery and murdered an innocent man. We can find the record of this account of lust, adultery and murder in the book of II Samuel. Don't fall into this age old scam. While living single you must grasp why it is important to wait and also recognize the benefits of serving God wholeheartedly. I know at one time or another the desire to give into the flesh can or will be overwhelming.

The Bible says, "Ye are of God, little children, and have overcome them: because greater is he that is in you, than he that is in the world" I John 4:4. We are able to sustain from temptations if we ask for God's help and stay out of risky situations. Be cautious in every area of your life. The enemy is looking to sexually entice singles from every angle. The devil uses television, music, internet, magazines, and friends from the past and present. Satan does not exclude anyone from his gimmicks of deceit. He is the father of deceit: "You belong to your father, the devil, and you want to carry out your father's desires. He was a murderer from the beginning, not holding to the truth, for there is no truth in him. When he lies, he speaks his native language, for he is a liar and the father of lies" John 8:44. The devil can't tell the truth and God can't lie. We will never resist temptation without higher help which only comes from the Lord.

Temptations are birthed from our past and present. Battles of temptation will come from angles we expect and least expect. The devil likes for us to reminisce on present temptations, past temptations and moments whereby we pleased your flesh. There will always be a test from the past given by the enemy. Satan remembers how a particular person made us feel. Satan remembers the vice-like grip God delivered us from. There may be new people in our life but the same old tricks from the past have a way of surfacing in our future. Satan knows the word of God better than any bible scholar. Satan has thousands of years of knowing the power of God, therefore; he will attempt to deceive anyone who takes his or her eyes off of the Lord. No one is exempt from a trial season. Every day we must make up in our mind to overpower the flesh.

The enemy misguides anyone who thinks they are able to conquer the flesh by their own will. Many people say they can't resist falling into temptation. They are absolutely correct in making that statement if God is not the head of their life. We can't resist the flesh without God. The power of God allows us to overpower the flesh. Power from God commands the flesh to act in accordance to His will. Power from God demands victory over the enemy. Becoming empowered by God causes bondages of the flesh to be broken. Strive daily to be free. Without a covering from God, there is no hope. Many people are losing their lives because they fail to defeat the flesh.

Many great men and women of God fell short in pleasing God because they rested for a period not realizing they didn't have on their full armor. It only takes one time for the flesh to be defeated. Prayerfully that one mistake won't be the death of you. Satan first sets up an opportunity for us to give into temptation. Then he hangs around to see if you fall into his trap. Don't ever think we are well over temptation on any level as a Christian. We must regard ourselves as dead in relation to sin, but alive in relationship with God, because we are in Christ Jesus. Singles constantly war in their flesh: therefore we must carry the word of God in our heart at all times. We must learn and apply the word of God every opportunity you get. Our flesh and character don't know each other. Don't deceive yourself thinking that a sinful nature is not a part of your character.

The Bible says, "Behold, I was shapen in iniquity; and in sin did my mother conceive me" Psalms 51:5. Flesh has no affiliation with Godly character. Flesh and character are not one in the same. Flesh and Godly character will never sit down and agree to join forces. Haven't you heard people on the news delivering bad news about an unfortunate event? Most often the perpetrator's family and friends state that the behavior demonstrated by their love one does not reflect his or her character. No one is excluded from trickery conducted by satan. Our character is developed through our upbringing and the life style we live. Morals are established from childhood. Principles for everyday living have been implanted. Satan does not recognize you, your values, morals, principles and keys for successful living. Satan is trying to come against persons who is Christ like. Satan is looking to destroy anyone who is striving to live holy.

Satan is in no position to judge morals and our belief system. Satan works along the line of a police sting. A police sting is a formulated operation to capture criminals. Satan is hoping that we will allow him to capture our mind and put our flesh in and under bondage. This is an imprisonment method that satan highly utilizes. Satan's tactics are deliberate and thoughtfully designed. It is a set up. If you are trying to catch a dog, then you are not going to give him cat food.

Satan is coming with something that is going to allure us; therefore it may not be obvious. We sin against our body and soul when we allow our desires to have full reign over our mind. As you consider the issue of how you are going to find a life partner remember that this is the will of God: that you abstain from fleshly lusts and from fornication, and that the will of God for you is your sanctification. Whatever way you go about finding a life partner, it must involve purity and chastity. Temptation presents itself often during the dating stages of singleness. Dating has a tendency to depend on romantic ideas rather than covenantal considerations.

In my experience I found out that romantic dates can be a great opportunity for satan to begin performing his tricks. Public places should be the focal localities for dating such as: restaurants, outings with friends and recreational dates. Secluded or romantic outings give the enemy latitude to execute at his best. When you make a decision to plan a romantic outing the devil takes a front seat in finding an opening to slither in for the kill. If you continue to think along the lines of continuous romance you increase your chances of falling prey to the enemy. Yes, there will be unplanned or planned romantic times, but don't taunt or tempt your flesh. Don't knowingly aim for a sensuous time which could possibly lead to the flesh being aroused. Many people have participated in making the enemy's job easier. Satan sits back a lot of the time and anticipates working to destroy us, but most often we find ways to destroy ourselves. Satan desires to work out his plan of destruction on all of us, but why bother when we self destruct on our own.

Many Christians and unbelievers give satan more credit than he deserves. We are our own worst enemy. Satan can't do anything until we permit him to do so. There are great men and women in the Bible who were caught off guard. Do you think their mind was protected when they fell into temptation? There are many Christians who were briefly distracted in their mind. The enemy strives on distractions. The enemy's first strategic attack is on the mind. Try fighting the spirit without positioning yourself under God's covering and you will be overpowered. The devil is subtle. We have to always be on guard: "Be on your guard; stand firm in the faith; be men of courage; be strong" I Corinthians 16:13. It is very essential that we learn spiritual techniques to protect ourselves. When tempted by satan we have to exercise daily crucifying the sinful nature of man. We will find it difficult at times to crucify the flesh when our sinful nature desires so much. We can't profess to have Jesus as the Lord of our life and the old man continues to indulge in fleshly desires. There has to be a renewing of our mind, heart and soul to resist temptation. Our feet can't tread on solid ground and sinking sand at the same time. It's impossible.

The Bible says, "What shall we say then? Shall we continue in sin, that grace may abound? God forbid. How shall we, that are dead to sin, live any longer therein? Know ye not, that so many of us as were baptized into Jesus Christ were baptized into his death? Therefore we are buried with him by baptism into death: that like as Christ was raised up from the dead by the glory of the Father, even so we also should walk in newness of life. For if we have been planted together in the likeness of his death, we shall be also in the likeness of his resurrection: Knowing this, that our old man is crucified with him, that the body of sin might be destroyed, that henceforth we should not serve sin. For he that is dead is freed from sin. Now if we be dead with Christ, we believe that we shall also live with him: Knowing that Christ being raised from the dead dieth no more; death hath no more dominion over him. For in that he died, he died unto sin once: but in that he liveth, he liveth unto God. Likewise reckon ye also yourselves to be dead indeed unto sin, but alive unto God through Jesus Christ our Lord. Let not sin therefore reign in your mortal body, that ye should obey it in the lusts thereof. Neither yield ye your members as instruments of unrighteousness unto sin: but yield yourselves unto God, as those that are alive from the dead, and your members as instruments of righteousness unto God. For sin shall not have dominion over you: for ye are not under the law, but under grace. What then? shall we sin, because we are not under the law, but under grace? God forbid. Know ye not, that to whom ye yield yourselves servants to obey, his servants ye are to whom ye obey; whether of sin unto death, or of obedience unto righteousness? But God be thanked, that ye were the servants of sin, but ye have obeyed from the heart that form of doctrine which was delivered you. Being then made free from sin, ye became the servants of righteousness. I speak after the manner of men because of the infirmity of your flesh: for as ye have yielded your members servants to uncleanness and to iniquity unto iniquity; even so now yield your members servants to righteousness unto holiness. For when ye were the servants of sin, ye were free from righteousness. What fruit had ye then in those things whereof ye are now ashamed?

for the end of those things is death. But now being made free from sin, and become servants to God, ye have your fruit unto holiness, and the end everlasting life. For the wages of sin is death; but the gift of God is eternal life through Jesus Christ our Lord" Romans 6: 1-23.

CHAPTER 5

WEAPONS OF WARFARE

Weapons - artillery for fighting.

Order ye the buckler and shield, and draw near to battle. Harness the horses; and get up, ye horsemen, and stand forth with your helmets; furbish the spears, and put on the brigandines. Jeremiah 46:3-4

We need weaponry in such a fierce battle with satan. We must invest in weapons that build up our spiritual man daily. We must in our salvation. We need power. I'm talking about Holy Ghost power. If we don't exercise the power that we have, we will lose it. If we lack power from God then seek it. Either we will fight the enemy with or without power. Regardless the enemy is going to fight us. Why not fuel up and top off constantly on God's power. There is no way we can win a war in our own strength. We can't tell the devil to exit our mind in our strength. Without God we have no power to resist temptation. Spirits of wickedness will overtake us. We can't handle the tremendous job of fighting the mind by ourselves. This job is beyond our control. We will never be competent for that job. Seek God for help. He is the only qualified candidate for the job. We can't fight in a war that is set up to be victorious without having a relationship with the Lord. There is no way we can fight the spirit of wickedness in our flesh. That attempt is hilarious to satan.

You have to fight the spirit of wickedness by the spirit of God. This method of defeating the enemy is our only way of surviving and winning this spiritual war. Recognize who we are fighting against and prepare a fierce attack in the spirit. When the enemy throws a fiery dart at us the word of God will combat it every time. The Bible says, "For the word of God is quick, and powerful, and sharper than any two-edged sword, piercing even to the dividing asunder of soul and spirit, and of the joints and marrow, and is a discerner of the thoughts and intents of the heart" Hebrews 4:12. This scripture is telling us that the word of God penetrates evenly and is powerful. The word of God is effective coming and going. Don't ever think we need more than the word of God to ward off satan. God and His word are more than sufficient. Battling the enemy while he attacks our mind entails stripping ourselves of the old man and renewing the mind. We have to renew our mind inwardly before there is a renewal on the outside. God wants full occupancy of our mind, so let Him have His way.

many of my dates and guess what happened? I fell into traps designed by satan and found myself in situations whereby God was displeased. My behavior exemplified ungodliness. If you observed me on particular dates you couldn't identify me as a follower of Christ or a member of satan's camp. My actions on some of these dates allowed me to blend in with the world. You don't ever want to be on a date that does not personify holiness. We must stand apart. If you fail to prepare to fight the enemy before dating you will experience great difficulties while dating. If you are not in a relationship, immediately invest the time to build up your spiritual man. If you are in a relationship strive to grow closer to God. Put forth your greatest efforts to be on one accord with God.

Allow God to reveal your strengths and weakness. Familiarize yourself with the dangers of dating. Whenever you begin dating temptation will surface. "Blessed is the man that endureth temptation: for when he is tried, he shall receive the crown of life, which the Lord hath promised to them that love him. Let no man say when he is tempted, I am tempted of God: for God cannot be tempted with evil, neither tempteth he any man. But every man is tempted, when he is drawn away of his own lust, and enticed. Then when lust hath conceived, it bringeth forth sin: and sin, when it is finished, bringeth forth death" James 1: 12-15. Make up your mind to please God on your dates. Remember God sits on the throne observing your every move and monitoring your thoughts whether they are righteous or unrighteous. You can endeavor to fool yourself. But God knows all. God is all knowing. I know there are some skeptics who differ on the dating perspective, but you are given orders from God to gird yourself and be separate from the world and its' thinking.

God has set standards for living holy. He requires holiness. On a date God wants you to reflect Him. I like the phrase, "What Would Jesus Do?" You have to be mindful about dating. Do you mirror God on your dates? As a servant of God you are under new management with new supervision. Your mind has been renewed. The manager in charge of you has your attention and as a good worker you should adhere to every word spoken by Him. Your stewardship has to change. Your new boss has a new way of thinking and performing. Your code of behavior changes from one manager to the next. Most often couples in the dating phase do not set out to displease God. It is a matter of losing focus or either a door was opened for the enemy to slip in. Satan does not need all the doors and windows open in a house to get in. All he requires is a small opening, crack, crevice, gap or cleft. Maybe the individuals who fall into sin did not recognize that there armor wasn't completely on. Maybe they carried the shield but lacked the helmet. Maybe they put on the breastplate of righteousness and forgot to shield their eyes. If you keep your mind on God, you will be protected from satan.

You can't afford to fall victim to the enemy in the area of dating. We have to conquer the flesh while dating. While dating you need to put limits on time spent with one another by yourselves. Don't fool yourself thinking you're so strong that you have it under control. That's the biggest scheme of the enemy. God wants you to be honest with yourself. You don't have anything under control. You can't even command a fly to fly. Sometimes you have good intentions to do right, but situations arise and you find it hard to resist temptation. Conquer the flesh or the flesh will conquer you. Listed below are a few scenarios of how the flesh can be conquered by way of a sly attack designed by satan.

1. Going out on a romantic date and the outcome is fornication. More than likely you didn't expect to have sex; therefore you and your date had unprotected sex. This one night of passion could warrant an unwanted disease (treatable or untreatable) or possibly a child could be conceived. In addition to being out of the will of God you're pregnant or have contracted a sexually transmitted disease.

2. You with your strong will self begin dating a man or woman who states they love the Lord, but they lack the fruits thereof. Yet you continue to date and the relationship evolves even more. You clearly see that the person you are dating is not committed to God like you thought or hoped he or she would be. Now you feel like there is a strong attachment to that individual and you can't release the involved party because of selfishness (wanting to please yourself). You are now torn between the man you love and God. This is dangerous!

3. Distraction is often developed when you meet someone that you are highly interested in; therefore

the enemy begins working overtime. Satan will work hard in the area of lust and fleshly interest. He attacks in this area because if lust is conceived in the mind, satan is hoping you will act on your thoughts and respond contrary to holiness. Satan knows if you can perceive ungodly thoughts then there is a possibility you will surrender to them. The devil favorably uses lust as a weapon of destruction and distraction.

The Bible says, "There is therefore now no condemnation to them which are in Christ Jesus, who walk not after the flesh, but after the Spirit. For the law of the Spirit of life in Christ Jesus hath made me free from the law of sin and death. For what the law could not do, in that it was weak through the flesh, God sending His own Son in the likeness of sinful flesh, and for sin, condemned sin in the flesh: That the righteousness of the law might be fulfilled in us, who walk not after the flesh, but after the Spirit. For they that are after the flesh do mind the things of the flesh; but they that are after the Spirit the things of the Spirit. For to be carnally minded is death; but to be spiritually minded is life and peace. Because the carnal mind is enmity against God: for it is not subject to the law of God, neither indeed can be. So then they that are in the flesh cannot please God. But ye are not in the flesh, but in the Spirit, if so be that the Spirit of God dwell in you. Now if any man has not the Spirit of Christ, he is none of his. And if Christ be in you, the body is dead because of sin; but the Spirit is life because of righteousness. But if the Spirit of him that raised up Jesus from the dead dwell in you, he that raised up Christ from the dead shall also quicken your mortal bodies by his Spirit that dwelleth in you. Therefore, brethren, we are debtors, not to the flesh, to live after the flesh. shall die: but if ye through the Spirit do mortify the deeds of the body, ye shall live. For as many as are led by the Spirit of God, they are the sons of God" Romans 8:1-14.

CHAPTER 9

THE WORLD'S TIME CLOCK

World – the earth or part of it, with its inhabitants and affairs.

For God so loved the world, that he gave His only begotten Son, that whosoever believeth in Him should not perish, but have everlasting life. For God sent not His Son into the world to condemn the world; but that the world through Him might be saved. **John 3:17**

You will never meet the time frame and dictates of the world. You don't have to be subject to the world and its mandates. Don't get caught up with the likes of the world. Satan is the prince of the world; therefore disregard his time clock and lies. You should not live a life of complaining about your clock. God has perfect timing for events to unfold in your life. Satan can't stop perfect timing. Satan is imperfect in timing and direction for your life. Will you allow man to develop a clock for you that does not match God's perfect timing? I can recall being infatuated with a man of God early in my walk with the Lord. I knew without a doubt this was going to be my husband. He loved the Lord and timing was perfect. He was so respectful towards women. His heart, time and money were centered on the Lord, and last but not least, he was very attractive. I know I was young in serving the Lord, but I was certain that this was a good man and the man for me. He was a minister.

He was a good man and a good looking man, but he wasn't the one God had for me. I couldn't understand why this relationship did not evolve into more. I thought this was perfect timing. I thought this was perfect timing for me to get married, have children and enjoy my husband. Why couldn't I have this man? It concerned me greatly. Let me reflect for a minute. When I wasn't living holy I thought I could capture any man that I wanted with my worldly ways. I couldn't grasp the understanding of a man not desiring to be with me. My philosophy was if I am interested in you, then you have to be interested in me. God had to clean up my way of thinking. God knew my mindset needed renewing. The carnal thinking I possessed needed to dissipate. I thought I was ready for a relationship, but God knew there was much more work needed on me. Now looking back on that stage of my life I appreciate the Lord for the process. Timing was not right. I thought since I was use to getting what I wanted from men in the world that the same would apply to obtaining a God fearing man.

My train of thinking had to dissolve. A man of God is not easily obtained. I'm not talking about a man who attends church faithfully. I'm not talking about a man who has been appointed to a position in the church, but lacking spiritual fruits. I'm talking about a man sold out for God. I'm talking about an anointed man of God. You should want a man that will not entangle himself with the likes of someone whom he finds attractive. A man or woman sold out for God will wait to hear from the Lord. A man or woman of God will attentively wait for God's permission to proceed with pursuing a relationship with you. God knows what you need at every stage of your life. I'm just guessing, you want the prize but don't like the race. Have you ever pondered on why timing has not permitted you all the things you sought or desired? It is because you're not ready. Yes you feel like you are ready, but God already knows what you are capable of handling. Many singles think they are ready for a relationship. God knows your future. Don't run this race without God controlling the clock. If you decide to step out on a limb without God you can almost guarantee a terrible fall.

Timing is important to God. The world's screwed up and miscalculated clock has no significance to your destiny. I can remember early in my walk thinking God was about to bless me with my mate because I stopped going out to clubs, drinking, fornicating, lying and stealing. I had a strong yearning to live an untainted life; therefore I definitely knew my mate would join me soon. There was no skepticism in my mind that my mate was not coming. I was determined to live right and knew for certain I was going to be rewarded. I believed I would receive immediate attention from God because in my mind I was doing well. Months of living holy went by and without reservation I strongly felt a change was happening in my situation. I believed that approaching change was a holy man entering my life. What's funny about this scenario is that I practiced this over and over in my head from one year to the next. Getting closer to God allowed me to stop dwelling on my situation and I began to enjoy being single.

God's life lessons equip His children to become empowered and complete. The enemy has an opportunity in this area of your life to make you think nothing will happen if you don't intervene with timing. Satan takes great delight in a single person professing to be happy yet they look sad and depressed because the clock the world has established is off track. Many people who know you may even question your character. They may think the reason you're not in a relationship is because of something you are doing is wrong. People are always watching and talking too much like the Pharisees. Don't get caught up with what others think of you. Sometimes, relationships are rushed into marriage because of what others think. Be comfortable about this golden time of your life. No matter what anyone says, you are complete and there is nothing wrong with you. I believe if you desire to be married then God will meet your request. God wants you to be happy, yet so many singles are sad and isolated because of singleness. Learn to appreciate total companionship with God. He loves the time and attention He receives from His children.

Sarai did not trust that God would meet her desire of having a child; therefore she intervened and requested her husband have a sexual relationship with their maidservant. Later she realized she acted prematurely, not knowing she would have a child. She found herself in a bitter situation for giving two willing parties permission to have sex and bare children: "Now Sarai, Abram's wife, had borne him no children. And she had an Egyptian maidservant whose name was Hagar. So Sarai said to Abram, "See now, the LORD has restrained me from bearing children. Please, go in to my maid; perhaps I shall obtain children by her." And Abram heeded the voice of Sarai. Then Sarai, Abram's wife, took Hagar her maid, the Egyptian, and gave her to her husband Abram to be his wife, after Abram had dwelt ten years in the land of Canaan. So he went in to Hagar, and she conceived. And when she saw that she had conceived, her mistress became despised in her eyes. Then Sarai said to Abram, "My wrong *be* upon you! I gave my maid into your embrace; and when she saw that she had conceived, I became despised in her eyes. The LORD judge between you and me." So Abram said to Sarai, "Indeed your maid *is* in your hand; do to her as you please." And when Sarai dealt harshly with her, she fled from her presence" Genesis 16:1-6.

This teaching reveals that there will always be problems when we make decisions without God. When you dart out before God you can expect sorrowful consequences. If you practice leaning on God and having confidence in Him you will experience great joy while on earth. Don't make any more mistakes. Trust God now. The process appears to be lengthy. But if you can hold out the results will be breathtaking. The race finished is more important than the beginning of the race.

I can recall attempting a three day fast with no food. I started off strong. I made it to the third morning. I knew my fast would be over by 3:00 pm. Before arriving to work I went to a local convenient store and picked up a candy bar. I had plans on eating the candy bar immediately after the fast was over. A few hours before the completion of the fast I gave into eating the candy bar. All I had was a few more hours and I did not hold out. I gave into the temptation to please my appetite.

The enemy planted a cowardice thought in my mind. It was an effort to make me give into the enticement to satisfy the hunger I felt. The devil planted a notion relaying it's not going to hurt you if you eat now; it's only a few hours. We must comprehend the importance of holding out to the end. The last hour of my fast was most critical in the completion of the fast. Satan does not want you to complete anything God's way. Followers of Christ could not hold on at the last hour. Disciples of Christ fell asleep during the last hour spent with Jesus: "And he cometh unto the disciples, and findeth them asleep, and saith unto Peter, What, could ye not watch with me one hour? Watch and pray, that ye enter not into temptation: the spirit indeed is willing, but the flesh is weak" Matthew 26:40-41. There is no room for slumber. It is not wise to doze off before the Lord's arrival. Satan loves an impatient person. Satan wants you to make hasty decisions without giving much attention or thought to consequences. Always remember that the devil is first at opposing God and His law.

You cannot get so wrapped up in your clock that you neglect serving God. There is peace in serving. There is unspeakable joy when serving. Serving is fulfilling. You have to make up your mind. Will you serve God or man? Once again the devil is attempting to fool people that he is a match to God. Satan will never match God in presenting good things to you. You must serve God all the days of your life. If that means in singleness, then that is how it shall be. If God blesses you with a mate, then that is how it shall be. If I didn't personally know the Lord I would have given into society's time frame for having children, getting married, obtaining a home and changing jobs. The world can't make you depressed over a situation that adores God. God adores the single man or woman because of their availability to work for Him. Even if it seems like you are off from the clock get back on track and serve God. Get the focus off of you and serve someone else. With every fiber in your body increase your efforts to please God. God has divine purpose for all of His children. There is life in singleness that must be celebrated by you. In other words seek to receive God's approval.

CHAPTER 10

REBUILDING FROM RUINS

Rebuilding – to repair; revise, reshape, or reorganize; to build again or refresh, to bring back into existence, use, or the like: state reestablish.

For all have sinned, and come short of the glory of God. **Romans 3:23**

Restoration begins with confessing your sin. Confession brings forgiveness and cleansing. "If we say that we have no sin, we deceive ourselves, and the truth is not in us. If we confess our sins, he is faithful and just to forgive us our sins, and to cleanse us from all unrighteousness. If we say that we have not sinned, we make Him a liar and His word is not in us" I John 1:8-10. Return to presence of the Lord. Restoration reconciles humanity back to God. God has the last word about restoration. God's plan is to redeem mankind and restore creation. God promised the Israelites a future Messiah who restores. Until Adam sinned, man had a perfect relationship with God. As a result of sin man fell. The relationship with God was severed. All of mankind is in need of Jesus restoring. Restoration begins with repentance.

In the Bible a prostitute was restored to holiness: "And early in the morning he came again into the temple, and all the people came unto him; and he sat down, and taught them. And the scribes and Pharisees brought unto him a woman taken in adultery; and when they had set her in the midst, They say unto him, Master, this woman was taken in adultery, in the very act. Now Moses in the law commanded us, that such should be stoned: but what sayest thou? This they said, tempting him, that they might have to accuse him. But Jesus stooped down, and with his finger wrote on the ground, as though he heard them not. So when they continued asking him, he lifted up himself, and said unto them, He that is without sin among you, let him first cast a stone at her. And again he stooped down, and wrote on the ground. And they which heard it, being convicted by their own conscience, went out one by one, beginning at the eldest, even unto the last: and Jesus was left alone, and the woman standing in the midst. When Jesus had lifted up himself, and saw none but the woman, he said unto her, Woman, where are those thine accusers? hath no man condemned thee? She said, No man, Lord. And Jesus said unto her, Neither do I condemn thee: go, and sin no more" John 8:2-11. This teaching reveals that no matter how great the sin, forgiveness is disbursed to all mankind.

A man possessed with demons was delivered by Jesus: "And when he was come to the other side into the country of the Gergesenes, there met him two possessed with devils, coming out of the tombs, exceeding fierce, so that no man might pass by that way. And, behold, they cried out, saying, What have we to do with thee, Jesus, thou Son of God? art thou come hither to torment us before the time? And there was a good way off from them an herd of many swine feeding. So the devils besought him, saying, If thou cast us out, suffer us to go away into the herd of swine. And he said unto them, Go. And when they were come out, they went into the herd of swine: and, behold, the whole herd of swine ran violently down a steep place into the sea, and perished in the waters. And they that kept them fled, and went their ways into the city, and told every thing, and what was befallen to the possessed of the devils. And, behold, the whole city came out to meet Jesus: and when they saw him, they besought him that he would depart out of their coasts" Matthew 8:28-34. Jesus demonstrates His power through the deliverance of demons. Whatever has an individual bound or shackled in sin, God can restore.

Whatever has you thinking, experimenting and or falling victim to sin is reason enough for restoration. Restoration comes in the form of cleaning, rebuilding, replacement, restoring functionality, loosening, tightening, stripping and patching holes. Satan practices hanging guilt over your head especially when you are striving to be restored. I fell down several times in my Christian walk. I will not make any excuse for falling. I fell into satan's trap, but I thank God so much for allowing me to get up. When I fell early in my Christian walk it didn't hurt me as much as it hurt me later since I knew God in greater way. Satan wants you to remain in a state where you feel guilty and defeated. If God says He forgives you, then take Him at His word and begin again. I didn't intentionally fall down. It was not planned. Once my fall into sexual sin occurred I immediately felt isolated and discouraged because I did not make it. I thought I would be that individual to hold out on having sex until I got married. Well I made a few mistakes and I beat myself up for weeks at a time.

Our heavenly Father forgives us right away when we ask for forgiveness, yet we are not as forgiving of ourselves. You will learn from your mistakes if you walk this single life in holiness. Well, I must say I am not Jesus, but I strive to be like Him daily. If you make a mistake get up and take your salvation by force. You will have critics until the day you die. People will continue to talk about you even after your death. Don't get caught up in how the world judges you. Those individuals judging probably forgot they were in the same boat years ago. But, oh how quick they forget about their past. Casting away what hinders your fellowship with God will lead to restoration. Transmit your burdens on the Lord "Cast thy burden upon the Lord, and he shall sustain thee: he shall never suffer the righteous to be moved" Psalm 55:22. When will you give it to God?

God says cast your cares on Him: "Cast your cares on the LORD and he will sustain you; he will never let the righteous fall" Psalm 55:22 (NIV). For some reason you give God a portion of your cares and you try to take care of the rest. You tend to be selective, giving God the problems that are overwhelming and you tackle the so-called insignificant ones. Let go and give it all to God. So many times you don't recognize the importance of letting go. There are wonderful things stored up for those who surrender it all to God. Is there anything in your life that is preventing you from getting closer to God? What must you give up or let go? This could be a friend from the past, addictions, lust, fornication, pornography, lying, stealing or any hindrance. Is it your old man mentality that God has to strip away? Is there something or somebody holding you back from doing what God has or is commanding you to do? Have you dropped everything to do God's will? Some people in your life will not go where God is trying to take you. This clearly means extra baggage is no longer needed on your journey.

If you have to let something go in order to serve God completely then let it go. There are blessings stored up for those who let something go. If it means ending a relationship with someone you love or care deeply for then make the necessary changes. I personally cared deeply about a man I knew I was unequally yoked with from the start. I had no choice but to do the right thing. I did love this man but spiritually we were not growing. He loved me, but he was not willing to serve God. He exercised another belief. This man could not understand why we could not remain together in a relationship. I knew from growing up under a God fearing mother and her biblical teachings that this relationship would not work. I can attest that breaking off this relationship was the hardest decision I had to make. I had been involved in a relationship with this man during my college years so it was difficult to end. I felt like I could not let all the history we shared dissolve, but I loved the Lord so much that I had to let him go. Did I shed some tears? Yes, a whole lot.

I greatly wanted this relationship to work, but nevertheless it didn't last. But now looking back there is nothing that compares to what I received from God for being obedient. Letting go of something that hinders your relationship with God shall be rewarded if you faint not. In the beginning of my Christian walk I was not sold out for the Lord. I grew up in a God fearing home so I was taught the truth about surrendering it all. Even though I knew about surrendering it all to serve God, I wasn't prepared to let go of some of my sinner man behaviors. The one thing that I was not willing to give up was my thinking about marriage. I heard about people waiting to have sex before marriage. My mother served God wholeheartedly, but she had sex before marriage. I knew great men and women of God that had sex before they married. The majority of holy people I knew had sex before marriage, so I thought this holding out until marriage concept was difficult. I thought if I tested the sexual waters before marriage, then I would know what I would be stuck with for the rest of my life.

God knew there was a lot of work to be done within me. I wasn't fully aware of the much needed spiritual reconstruction that my mind and spirit required. I thank God every day for intervening on my behalf. Looking back on my past and even looking ahead into the future I thank God for His mercy and grace. Whatever you leave behind makes room for what lies ahead. When you refuse to drop everything that is offensive to your soul it will eventually manifest itself into destruction. Whatever is hindering you from walking out your destiny rid yourself of it. I know personally about letting go of something that had no connection to the Lord. I loved the Lord so much that I had no choice. I had to walk away from this relationship. When it comes to the Lord let nothing hinder your relationship. Let nothing separate you from being with the Lord wholeheartedly. I will profess and tell you it wasn't easy. I had weeks of astounding pain, but as time went by and being in constant fellowship with God, He got me through.

Letting go of something dear to you is never going to be easy. If you were able to peak into your future, you would release whatever is necessary to carry out God's plan. By all means release what is hindering your spiritual growth. Put the past behind you. Walking with God requires moving forward without looking backwards. The outcome for looking back is never rewarded. Lot, his wife and children were instructed to not look back in the bible, but his wife looked backed and her end was determined: "But his wife looked back from behind him, and she became a pillar of salt" Genesis 19:26. Looking backwards will have you stuck in the past. Your future is greater. Have you ever seen an Olympian run in the Olympics backwards? Most competitions are performed moving forward or by masterfully adhering to the criteria of pressing forward. You can't move forward in Christ until there is a removal of self. You have to step aside and patiently wait. Your temple in this journey is for renovation. God wants a place of habitation.

Is there a thorn in your life? The thorn is indicative of the opposition in your life. Thorns keep you humble and very useful to God. Wanting a thorn to be removed does not give you an opportunity to get closer to God. Messenger of satan pricked Paul with a thorn in his flesh. This thorn did not come from God. Paul asked God to take this thorn out of his life. In response God told Paul he would give him the grace and strength to deal with the problem. Paul then said he would boast in infirmities, reproaches, needs, persecutions and distresses, all the while depending on God for strength: "And lest I should be exalted above measure through the abundance of the revelations, there was given to me a thorn in the flesh, the messenger of Satan to buffet me, lest I should be exalted above measure. For this thing I besought the Lord thrice, that it might depart from me. And he said unto me, My grace is sufficient for thee: for my strength is made perfect in weakness. Most gladly therefore will I rather glory in my infirmities, that the power of Christ may rest upon me. Therefore I take pleasure in infirmities, in reproaches, in necessities, in persecutions, in distresses for Christ's sake: for when I am weak, then am I strong" II Corinthians 12:7-10. Surrender to God your will regardless of the thorn in your flesh.

Focus on ongoing restoration to your spiritual building. Whatever prevents rebuilding and restoration get rid of it and pursue God intensely. Are you a bad person when you fall prey to the enemy? Of course not, but God is displeased. Jesus forgives the repentant man: "Let the wicked forsake his way and the evil man his thoughts. Let him turn to the Lord, and he will have mercy on him, and to our God, for he will freely pardon" Isaiah 55:7. For a restoring moment such as this God knew you would need a Savior: to get you out of a jam; to remove your burdens; hurts; to encourage you and support you. The first step in rebuilding is recognizing the sin that exist and repenting for it.

The book of Nehemiah teaches us the principles of rebuilding from ruins. Nehemiah was a man that knew how to get results and that was by getting into the presence of God for direction. Nehemiah received word from a kinsman that Jerusalem was desolated and he wept. Shortly afterward he began praying and fasting. Jerusalem weighed heavily on Nehemiah in such a way that he sought out help from the only source to deliver him from weariness. Nehemiah sought out help from God. Nehemiah did not move hastily to fix a situation. He waited until the time was right. During the restoration period he experienced opposition.

Nehemiah experienced ridicule, troublemakers, discouragement from within his camp, distractions, intimidations and false accusations. Despite the oppositional process Nehemiah and his brethren completed the task of rebuilding in 52 days. It does not take God years to move on your behalf. Put a plan of action in place for your relationship. If you've fallen into sexual sin or ungodly acts stop now and begin building up from ground level. Whereby it appears that the relationship is beyond repair God is able to restore. God will reconstruct a relationship if both parties involved are on one accord to be restored to holiness. You can't build with one opposing party in play.

An opposing party in your relationship will have you disobeying the will of God. A couple without God leading the way faces a lifestyle of strain. Strain in a relationship can be prevented with proper planning and assistance from God. Most believers who are walking holy and single will encounter during the single and holy season periods of the flesh desiring to be satisfied, but God will always sustain you if you turn it completely into His hands. You will find it highly difficult to resist temptation if you continue to flirt with matters that involve the flesh directly. You must move forward if you've engaged or are engaged in acts that God hates? Stop right now and repent. Repenting is your weapon of defense. You do not want to become as someone who is religious who exercises repenting before the sinful act. Knowing what sin you will partake in and repenting immediately thereafter is dangerous. God does not play games. This is not true repentance. Sincerely repent and began fighting harder than ever before. Fight with a determination to win.

You are combating for your life. Don't lean on the ropes barely hanging in there. If you get knocked down fight to get up. You don't have to stay there. Early on and later on in my walk with God I experienced falling prey to temptation. At one point in my life I became frustrated and sin seeped in. Many people whom I surrounded myself would have never known that I was struggling everyday with my flesh like most people. I thank God for His mercy and for every test given whether I passed them right away or not. If you continue to fall into sin then you must ask yourself what or who is present in your life that contributes to your spiritual downfall. Make a sound decision to suppress your flesh. God cannot provide help for you if you don't call on Him. Falling down produces a reaction called getting up. If you fall down, do not remain in a fallen state. Get up and regain momentum for the next tactic. It would be better for you to change direction than to remain in the situation that God abhors.

God is a merciful God and He allows you to getup. Thank God for resurrection abilities. You have to make up your mind and tell satan enough is enough. You have to stop falling vulnerable to his tricks and lean not on yourself to win battles. You have to literally lie prostrate at God's feet and ask for help. You can't live a successful single life without completely conceding to God.

Don't try this season of singleness without the Lord. Don't try this season with less power than the previous season. Each season is greater than the next. Satan is fully aware that you are spiritually progressing and he wants to put an end to you and your life. Therefore; satan will invent plans to aide in your downfall if he has a chance. Rebuilding from ruins will manifest rewards if you endure the task. Deciding to do things God's way will allow you to reap great rewards. Rewards are accomplished by having determination. Having strong desires and fixations on a purpose releases maximum outcomes. Will you give God the opportunity to wow you? God takes great delight in blessing His children.

God wants to reward you for obedience. Satan does not know anything about rewards. Full obedience guarantees a life in the overflow with God. There are many rewards for obedience during the rebuilding period. Scripture states that for every one that asketh receiveth; and he that seeketh findeth and to him that knocketh it shall be opened. If a son shall ask bread of any you that is a father, will he give him a stone? Or if he ask a fish, will he for a fish give him a serpent? Or if he shall ask an egg, will he offer him a scorpion? If ye then, being evil, know how to give good gifts unto your children how much more shall your heavenly Father give the Holy Spirit to them that ask him?" Luke 11: 9-13.

Can you believe that God delights in given you the desires of your heart? There are rewards, gifts and blessings that God has secured specifically for all that desire to rebuild by following God's word. When you fail to take heed to instructions from God you will regret the decision you make without Him. You must include God in all decision making and actions. If you want the blessings of God on your life then serve and keep Him ahead of you for direction. God did reward me with a wonderful man. God lead me through singleness and now is guiding me in marriage. Living holy and single for the Lord will reap unprecedented spiritual promotions and rewards. God has astounded me in singleness and I assure you that He will do the same for you.